Gold

Anita Louise McCormick

Enslow Publishing
101 W. 23rd Street
Suite 240
New York, NY 10011
USA
enslow.com

Published in 2019 by Enslow Publishing, LLC.
101 W. 23rd Street, Suite 240, New York, NY 10011

Library of Congress Cataloging-in-Publication Data

Names: McCormick, Anita Louise, author.
Title: Gold / Anita Louise McCormick.
Description: New York : Enslow Publishing, [2019] | Series: Exploring the elements | Audience: Grades 5 to 8. | Includes bibliographical references and index.
Identifiers: LCCN 2018009578 | ISBN 9781978503656 (library bound) | ISBN 9781978505407 (paperback)
Subjects: LCSH: Gold—Juvenile literature. | Periodic table of the elements—Juvenile literature.
Classification: LCC QD181.A9 M33 2018 | DDC 546/.656—dc23
LC record available at https://lccn.loc.gov/2018009578

Printed in the United States of America

To Our Readers: We have done our best to make sure all website addresses in this book were active and appropriate when we went to press. However, the author and the publisher have no control over and assume no liability for the material available on those websites or on any websites they may link to. Any comments or suggestions can be sent by email to customerservice@enslow.com.

Photo Credits: Cover, p. 1 (chemical element symbols) Jason Winter/Shutterstock.com; cover, p. 1 (gold nuggets) optimarc/Shutterstock.com; p. 5 Bettmann/Getty Images; p. 8 Fritz Prenzel/Photolibrary/Getty Images; p. 11 AlexLMX/Shutterstock.com; p. 12 BlueRingMedia/Shutterstock.com; p. 15 udaix/Shutterstock.com; p. 17 trgrowth/Shutterstock.com; p. 18 Dimitar Dilkoff/AFP/Getty Images; p. 21 Jiri Vaclavek/Shutterstock.com; p. 22 hispan/Shutterstock.com; p. 25 Arsel Ozgurdal/Shutterstock.com; p. 31 Colin Hawkins/The Image Bank/Getty Images; p. 32 Anadolu Agency/Getty Images; p. 34 WENN Ltd/Alamy Stock Photo; p. 37 lapas77/Shutterstock.com; p. 39 schankz/Shutterstock.com.

Contents

Introduction

G old is one of the most valuable elements on the planet. You have probably heard the term "gold standard" when someone wants to describe something as being the best in its class.

Many currency systems in the world are based on gold because everyone knows gold has a high value. In ancient times, gold coins were used for buying and selling. In today's world, while gold coins still exist, many nations, including the United States, use paper money. But paper money only has value because it represents gold or other precious metals that are held in a storehouse.

In the 1930s, during World War II, the United States government decided to use Fort Knox, KY, as the United States Bullion Depository.

Fort Knox became a place to hold the United States' gold reserve and guarantee the value of our nation's paper money. In today's market, the gold in Fort Knox is worth approximately $130 billion.

As with many other elements, much of the gold we have on our planet originated in space. Scientists have determined that nearly

Fort Knox, an army base in Kentucky, is where the United States stores a large portion of its gold bullion supply.

four billion years ago, long before humans inhabited Earth, a meteor shower brought large quantities of gold and other precious metals to Earth. At that time, Earth's crust was still in the process of being formed, and frequent meteor showers, earthquakes, and volcano eruptions were common. Earth's land mass was still developing, and scientists have determined the only life that could have survived in such an unstable climate were tiny microbes.

Elements make up everything in space and on Earth, as well as everything humans have built or manufactured. Elements make up the planets of our solar system, the air we breathe, the ground we walk on, our own human bodies, and the water and food we need to stay healthy. Some of these elements exist in pure form, while others exist mostly as molecules, which are made up of various elements. When elements form molecules, they have different properties than any of the elements they are made of. Those properties are unique to the type of molecule they form. For example, as individual elements, hydrogen and oxygen are gasses. But when two hydrogen atoms and one oxygen atom combine, they make water.

There are at least 118 known elements in the universe. They include metals, nonmetals, inert gasses, and metalloids.

Gold, the element you are learning about in this book, can be found in many places. If you go into a jewelry store, you can find gold in earrings, necklaces, and fancy watches. Olympic athletes compete for medals that are plated with gold—the last medals that were solid gold were awarded in 1912. Other places you can find gold might surprise you. For example, many cell phones, computers, and other technical devices have small amounts of gold inside them to protect electrical connections.

Scientists estimate that the world's oceans contain more than 10,000,000 tons (9,000,000 metric tons) of gold. Unfortunately, it is in very low concentrations—for every hundred billion parts of ocean, there is only one part gold. The concentration is so low that it would cost more than the gold would be worth to extract it.

The goal of this book is to help you understand more about gold and its fascinating history.

Understanding the Atom

//

H umans have known about and used gold since ancient times. Archeologists tell us that prehistoric man probably discovered the bright flakes and nuggets of gold in streams and river beds. Early civilizations in many parts of the world collected gold and learned how to work with it. Archaeologists have unearthed gold jewelry made by skilled craftsmen in Egypt that is over 5,000 years old. The first gold coins that archeologists are aware of appeared about 2,500 years ago in Asia Minor, an area that today is part of Turkey.

For much of history, gold was regarded as a valuable metal. But until the modern scientific age, it was not considered an element. Early chemists, known as alchemists, believed that gold and other metals were mixtures of the four fundamental elements —earth,

Gold has been known to humans since antiquity. Egyptians, Romans, and Greeks all used this valuable metal.

air, water, and fire. By changing the proportion of these four elements, alchemists believed they could turn one metal into another. The key to this transformation was a magical substance called the philosopher's stone. However, there is no such thing as the philosopher's stone. The alchemists' quest to create gold out of less valuable metals was bound to fail.

By the eighteenth century, the four-element theory had been discarded. Instead, scientists began defining an element as any substance that could not be broken down into simpler substances. Water was not an element because it could be broken down into two other substances, hydrogen and oxygen. Other suspected elements were treated to a barrage of tests. They were heated and cooled, jolted with electricity, doused with acid, pounded, and filtered. If the sample broke down into something else, it was not an element. Gold, however, was an element.

What Makes Up the Elements?

By the nineteenth century, scientists had started to suspect that the elements were made of tiny individual particles, which they called atoms. The bulk of experiments to test this theory involved using highly sensitive equipment, so scientists could carefully weigh the amount of each element that combines to form a compound.

In one famous experiment, John Dalton, a chemist from England, weighed carbon and oxygen that reacted to form two different compounds. He found that twice as much oxygen combined with the same amount of carbon in one compound compared to the other. This result could only be explained if one of the compounds was made out of twice as many atoms of oxygen as the other compound. Additional experiments supported this theory. These experiments provided solid evidence that elements were made from a basic unit, or building block, otherwise known as the atom.

However, there was still one unanswered question: If the elements were made from atoms, then what made up the atoms? By the early twentieth century, scientists had found the answer to this question. They discovered that atoms are made of three smaller particles: electrons, protons, and neutrons.

What Are Protons?

Protons are positively charged. Together with neutrons, they form the center of the atom, which is known as the nucleus. The nucleus is incredibly small, but also incredibly dense. If a gold nucleus were the size of a pea, it would weigh 250,000,000 tons (230,000,000 metric tons).

The number of protons in an atom determines the element. For example, an atom of gold always has seventy-nine protons. Take away one proton and you don't have gold anymore—you have platinum. Add one proton to the atom and you have the element mercury.

What Are Neutrons?

Neutrons do not have a positive or negative charge. They are neutral. They act as the glue of the nucleus, keeping all the particles bound tightly. Without the neutrons, the protons would not be able to get close to one another. This is because protons are positively charged, and particles with the same charge repel each other, or push each other away. The neutrons work by stepping between the protons and neutralizing their repulsive forces.

What Are Electrons?

Electrons are negatively charged particles. They are attracted to the positively charged protons in the nucleus. The electrons dart around outside the nucleus in what are known as orbitals, or shells. Electrons are much lighter than protons and neutrons. They contribute very little to the mass of an atom.

An atom can have anywhere from one to seven shells of electrons. Each shell is progressively farther away from the nucleus. Electrons in the inner shells are held very tightly by the attractive forces of the protons in the nucleus. The electrons in the outer shells are held less tightly.

Gold at a Glance

Chemical Symbol: Au
Classification: Transition metal
Discovered By: Known since prehistoric times
Atomic number: 79
Atomic Weight (actual): 196.966
Protons: 79
Electrons: 79
Neutrons: 118
Density at 68°F (20°C): 19.3 g/cm³
Melting Point: 1,948°F; 1,064°C

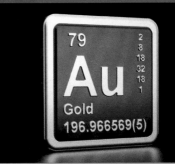

Gold's atomic number is 79, making it one of the higher numbered elements that occur naturally.

Boiling Point: 5,173°F; 2,856°C
Other properties: conducts electricity, malleable, ductile
Commonly Found: In stream or river beds, Earth's crust, soil, oceans

Gold Atoms

Every atom of gold contains 79 protons, 79 electrons, and 118 neutrons. The number of protons and electrons are equal in order to balance out the opposite charges of the two particles. When the two particles are not balanced, the atom is said to be an ion. An ion is an atom, or cluster of atoms, that has either gained or lost elec-

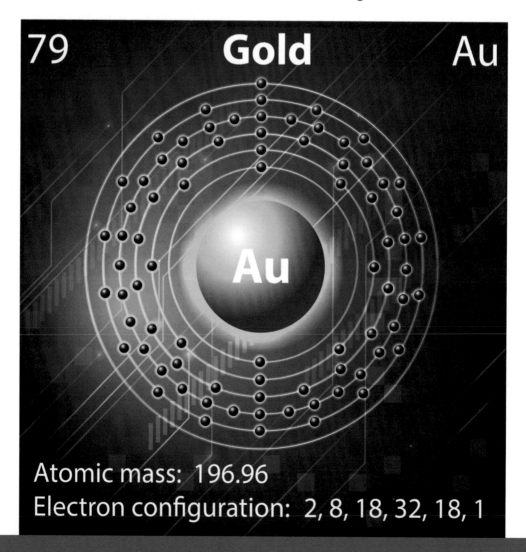

79   **Gold**   Au

Au

Atomic mass: 196.96
Electron configuration: 2, 8, 18, 32, 18, 1

The element of gold, showing how its
79 electrons are arranged

trons. An ion has a positive charge if it has lost one or more electrons and a negative charge if it has gained one or more electrons. For example, a gold atom that has lost three electrons is an ion with a charge of +3.

Gold has six shells of electrons. The first shell has two electrons, while there are eight in the second, eighteen in the third, thirty-two in the fourth, and eighteen in the fifth. The sixth and outer shell has only one electron.

Chemical Bonding in Elements

The outer shell electrons, also known as valence electrons, are of special interest to chemists. These electrons are involved in chemical bonding, which occurs when two or more atoms join together. When atoms of different elements bond, they form a compound. Water, salt, and sugar are a few examples of compounds..

Gold has one outer shell electron. Often, elements with only one electron in their outer shell are very reactive and easily combine with other elements to form compounds. This is true of such elements as sodium, potassium, and lithium. However, gold's relatively large nucleus exerts a strong pull on the lone electron in the outer shell, so the electron is pulled in very tight. Because of this, that electron is usually not made available for bonding. This tendency of gold to hold tight to its outer shell electron largely determines its chemical properties.

2

The Periodic Table—a Map of the Elements

///

n 1869, Dmitri Mendeleev, a Russian chemistry professor, created the first periodic table of the elements. His table arranged the known elements by weight, from lightest to heaviest. He included the table in a chemistry textbook to help his students recognize patterns in how the elements behaved

Although today's periodic table has been revised and expanded many times since the days of Mendeleev, the table's basic appearance is still the same. Each element is given a one-, two-, or three-letter symbol. Usually, the symbol is an abbreviation of the element's name in English—H, for example, stands for hydrogen. Gold's symbol is a bit unusual. Its symbol is Au, short for *aurum*, which is what gold is called in Latin. A few of the other

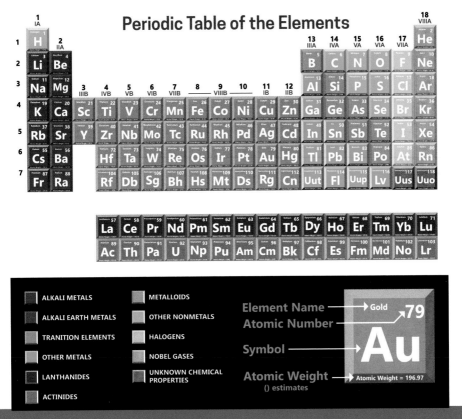

Gold is a transition metal and a group 11 element.
It is the most malleable of all metals.

elements, like iron (Fe) and sodium (Na), also use symbols based on their Latin names, *ferrum* and *natrium*.

The elements in the table are arranged in rows, known as periods, and columns, known as groups. The periods are numbered one to seven from top to bottom. The groups are numbered in one of two ways, depending on what version of the table you are using. In the first numbering system, the groups are numbered from one to eighteen going left to right. In the second, each group is given a Roman numeral followed by a letter. For example, gold is in group IB, while sulfur is in group VIA.

Below the main table is a smaller table made up of two rows and fourteen columns. This block is part of the main table, but has been cut out so the table can fit on a single piece of paper. The first row of the smaller table should go on the main table in between Lanthanum (atomic number 57) and Hafnium (atomic number 72). The second row of the smaller table goes between Actinium (atomic number 89) and Rutherfordium (atomic number 104).

The Element Groups

Elements that are grouped together often have similar chemical properties. This means that they react with other elements or compounds in similar ways. The elements in the first two columns react with elements in column VIIA to form a type of compound called a salt. Table salt, or sodium chloride (NaCl), is the best known of the salts.

Some of the groups of the table have been given special names. The elements in the first column are known as the alkali metals, and the elements in the second column are known as the alkaline earth metals, while the elements in column VIIA are known as the halogens. The far right column of the table consists of the noble gases. This group is unique because they never react with other elements.

Other than gold, the transition metals group includes iron, nickel, copper, zinc, and silver.

Gold belongs to a block of elements called the transition metals. These elements form the middle of the table, from the third column to the twelfth column. These elements do not share chemical properties as neatly as other groups such as the halogens, alkali metals, or noble gases. Within the transition metals, even within the same column, the elements can have vastly different chemical properties. They do, however, have some things in common. The transition metals can conduct electricity and heat. They can also be twisted into wires and pounded into sheets. Besides gold, the transition metals group includes iron, nickel, copper, zinc, and silver.

Numbers on the Table

If you look at any square on the periodic table, you will see two numbers. The smaller number is the atomic number, which is equal to the number of protons in an atom of the element. For gold, the atomic number is 79, which means an atom of gold has 79 protons. Copper has an atomic number of 29, and therefore an atom of copper has

There's Silver in Your Gold Medal!

Every four years, Olympic athletes gather from around the world to compete for gold, silver, and bronze medals in their sports. For the 2018 South Korean games, less than 50 ounces of gold was used to make all of the gold medals handed out to competitors. In 1912, the medals were still solid gold,

The gold medals given out at the Olympics are actually thin coatings of gold over a medal that's mostly silver.

but modern gold medals are silver plated with gold—about six grams of it. Beneath that six grams of gold is silver said to be 99.99% pure. Each gold medal weighs in at 586 grams (20 ounces).

At the 2018 price for gold, around $1,314 an ounce, the total value of the gold used in the South Korean medals was around $65,700.

29 protons. Unless the atom is an ion, the atomic number also indicates the number of electrons.

If you scan the table, you should notice that the elements are arranged from left to right by their atomic numbers. The element with an atomic number of one (hydrogen) is in the upper left hand square. Ununoctium, the element with the largest atomic number, is in the bottom right square.

In each square of the table, the larger number is the atomic weight (also known as atomic mass). The atomic weight is the average weight of an atom of the element. It is measured in what are known as atomic mass units (amu). Gold has an atomic weight of 196.966 amu.

Atomic weight is an average weight and not an exact weight.

This is because elements are not always made from identical atoms. Often, they consist of isotopes, which are atoms with the same number of protons but different numbers of neutrons. Carbon, for example, has three naturally occurring isotopes. The most common isotope of carbon has twelve neutrons, while another has thirteen neutrons. A third isotope has fourteen neutrons. The atomic weight is the average weight of all these isotopes, taking into consideration how often each isotope occurs. Gold is somewhat unusual because it has only one naturally occurring isotope, which always has 118 neutrons.

How We Can Use the Periodic Table

The periodic table is a compact and convenient chart that provides a great deal of basic information about each of the elements. You can see protons, electrons, and determine the number of electron shells that an element has.

The table arranges the elements into groups, which means you can know a lot about an element by its location in the table. Gold is located in the transition metal block, so you can assume that gold will have some properties shared by transition metals. Properties of transition metals include the ability to conduct electricity and heat, have a shiny surface, and can be pulled into wires and pounded into sheets.

3

Understanding the Properties of Gold

//

S uppose you worked in a chemistry lab. One day, your boss gave you an envelope containing a small metal cube that is believed to be gold to test. How would you go about testing the metal cube to find out if it was truly gold?

First, you would need to investigate the properties of the sample. In science, "property" is another way of saying "characteristic," or "trait." It is something that distinguishes one thing from another. Properties can be measured or observed. They include qualities such as an element's density, melting point, and color. By measuring and observing the properties of your sample, you would be able to determine if it is gold or something else.

Is this gold-colored sample really gold?
We can run tests to find out!

Visual Identification of Elements

What does it look like? Properties you should note include color, texture, and whether it is a solid, liquid, or gas. If your sample is gold, it should be a golden yellow color, have a shiny surface, and be solid. If it doesn't have these properties, you can be pretty sure it is not gold.

However, just because it looks like gold doesn't mean you are finished with your examination. It could easily be something that only looks like gold—so more tests will be required.

What Does It Mean for an Element to Be a Metal?

Gold, like all metals, can conduct electricity and heat, be pounded into sheets, and be stretched into wires. Your next test should confirm that your sample has all these qualities.

This microprocessor uses gold because gold is a great conductor of electricity.

Electrical and Thermal Conductivity of Gold

Gold can conduct electricity because its outer-shell electrons can move easily from atom to atom. When electricity is applied, the electrons create an electrical current. The electrical conductivity of gold can be measured in the laboratory using a battery and an ammeter, a device that measures electricity.

Gold will also conduct heat, which is known as thermal conductivity. One simple way to test thermal conductivity is to measure how fast an object heats up once it comes into contact with a hot object or liquid.

Imagine that you have a cup made of gold and a cup made of glass. If you were to pour boiling water into each, the gold cup would heat more quickly than the glass cup. This is because metals conduct heat much better than glass.

Malleability of Gold

Malleability means that a substance can be pounded into sheets or bent into different shapes. A diamond (pure carbon), for example, is not malleable. When it is struck, it will not flatten, nor can it be bent with any instrument. Most metals, including gold, are malleable. This explains why an element like aluminum can be turned into foil, or why silver can be shaped into a medallion. Gold is the most malleable of all the elements. It can be pounded into sheets one thousand times thinner than a human hair!

If your sample can be hammered into something softer and flatter, you might have gold. If it shatters, you can tell your boss the sample was not gold.

Ductility of Gold

Gold is the most ductile of the elements. Ductility is the ability to be stretched into wires. Copper is another example of a ductile element. This property, along with its ability to conduct electricity, makes copper a popular choice for electrical wiring. Gold also makes excellent electrical wire, but since it is so expensive, it is not widely used for this purpose.

If you had wire-making equipment in your laboratory, you could test your sample and see how well it can be stretched into a thin piece of wire.

Melting Points Help Identify Elements

An element's melting point is often used to help scientists distinguish between two substances. The melting point is the temperature at which a substance changes from the solid phase to the liquid phase.

Melting points can vary radically from element to element and between different substances. The melting points of metallic elements range from mercury at –36° Fahrenheit (–38° Celsius) to tungsten at 6,170° F (3,410° C). Gold falls somewhere in between, with a melting point of 1,948° F (1,064° C).

Gold melts at 1,948° F, so any gold you have around the house should be pretty safe from random melting!

A temperature of nearly 2,000° F (1,093° C) is much hotter than what you can reach in your oven at home. But imagine that your high-tech laboratory has a furnace that can reach temperatures of 2,000° F. Place your sample in the furnace and turn up the heat. If it melts at any temperature other than 1,948° F [1,064° C], give or take a few degrees, you will know that your sample is not gold.

Gold Is a Dense Element

Density is the measurement of weight per volume. An element that is dense has a lot of weight packed into a small space. Gold is a dense element because of two things: the weight of each individual atom and the way those atoms are packed together.

Gold's large nucleus of 79 protons and 118 neutrons has a strong effect on the surrounding electrons, pulling them in very tight. The result is a tightly packed and very heavy atom.

But your sample of gold is more than just one atom—it's a collection of many atoms. In fact, a piece of gold the size of a grain of rice contains billions of atoms. Gold's density is also a result of all these atoms arranging themselves in tightly packed structures.

To measure density in the laboratory, you need to weigh the sample using an accurate scale. Then, you measure the sample's volume.

The Archimedes' Principle

Archimedes was a Greek mathematician, engineer, and inventor (287–212 BCE). It is said he was asked to determine whether a crown made for a king was actual gold, or made in part with silver. Archimedes was instructed to make the calculation without destroying the crown, which meant he could not melt it down to determine what it was made of. When getting in and out of his bath, Archimedes realized the level of water rose and fell, and he could use the crown in a similar way, to see how much water it displaced. By dividing the mass of the crown by the volume of water displaced, he could know the density of the crown.

Dividing the mass by the volume gives you the sample's density. If the sample is gold, its density should be about 19.3 grams per cubic centimeter.

Chemical Reactions of Gold

Another way to test an element is to see how it reacts with other elements or compounds. Gold is unique because it does not react with water, air, most acids, and almost anything else. In fact, gold is one of the least reactive of all the elements.

Gold does not react easily because of the tight grip each atom has on its outer electron. When atoms of other elements pass by looking for electrons to grab and bond with, they are turned away. Atoms of gold would rather bond with each other than with atoms of any of the other elements.

Try mixing your sample with water, acid, alcohol, laundry detergent, salt, soda pop, or anything you want. If it is gold, then none of these substances will change your sample.

Discoveries and Uses of Gold

Throughout human history, gold has been highly valued. One reason is because gold is so rare. If you were to rank the elements from most abundant to least abundant, gold would be seventy-third out of the 118 currently known elements.

The physical and chemical properties of gold also make it desirable. Its color and reflective surface make gold visually appealing. Since it is malleable and ductile, artists and craftsmen can take a nugget of gold and shape it into something even more beautiful. Gold does not react with air, water, and most other substances, so gold does not corrode, rust, or otherwise change over time. Gold will look exactly the same in one hundred years as the day it was purchased.

Gold's value has led many to go to great lengths to retrieve it from the earth. It is not easy to find, so it takes special skills, equipment, and a lot of patience and hard work to find it.

Where Can We Find Gold?

People who search for gold are known as prospectors. They look for gold in two places—within Earth's crust and at the bottom of its streams and rivers. Sections of Earth's crust with high concentrations of gold are known as veins. A vein with an exceptionally high concentration of gold is called a lode.

Gold veins form when hot fluids rise within Earth and dissolve gold lodged in rock. When the fluid finds a crack in the rock, it begins to cool. As a result, gold and other minerals are released, forming gold-rich veins. The gold lodged inside a vein can vary in size from small grains, to flakes, to larger chunks called nuggets. Often, the minerals quartz and pyrite are also found with the gold.

When a river or stream passes over a gold vein, some of the gold is washed away. This process is called erosion. The gold that is washed away is deposited downstream along with sand and gravel. Over time, the gold grains and flakes collect in the river or stream bed. These areas are known as placer deposits.

Until 2006, South Africa lead the world in gold production, but as of 2016, Asia leads the world, producing 455 metric tons of gold per year. South Africa's Witwatersrand placer deposit once produced as much as 40 percent of the world's gold, but it's the Grasberg mine in Indonesia that holds the rank as the world's largest as of 2018.

Panning for Gold

The first prospectors found their gold in placer deposits. Working in rivers or stream beds, they used pans to scoop up water, sand, and gravel. When they swirled the contents of their pans, the less dense sand and gravel spilled out with the water. Since gold is heavier, it remained at the bottom of the pan.

Panning is a simple technique that can be done by a single prospector and does not require any fancy equipment. Because of this, panning has been popular throughout history, including during the famous California gold rush of the mid-nineteenth century.

Mining Gold from Rocks

Removing gold from rocks is a much more difficult process. It requires much more sophisticated equipment than panning. Gold-bearing rock, called ore, is dug out of the earth for cyanidation—that's one way of extracting gold from rock.

In the first step of cyanidation, machinery crushes the ore. Then a compound called cyanide is added, along with oxygen and water. The carbon and nitrogen in cyanide combines with the gold to create an ion that dissolves in the water. The rest of the ore does not dissolve in the water and can be discarded.

At this point, you have gold bound to cyanide and dissolved in water, which isn't very useful. How can the gold be recovered? By adding a metal that the cyanide bonds with more easily than gold. For example, when zinc is added to the water, the cyanide lets go

Gold prospectors dig their pans into riverbeds, sifting through silt and debris, looking for gold.

Gold miners working in an African gold mine. How can gold be removed from rock? Cyanidation is one method.

of the gold and attaches to the zinc. Gold is released and collects on the bottom of container, much like panning.

Cyanidation may be effective, but it is also destructive to the environment. Cyanide is a dangerous chemical and can be fatal if ingested by humans. When used in gold mining, it can contaminate streams, rivers, and lakes Many environmental groups are calling for a ban on cyanide use in gold mining. In the United States, Montana has already banned its use, as has the country of Turkey.

Bacteria Can Be Used to Extract Gold

Another method of obtaining gold uses rock-eating bacteria. These tiny critters feed on pyrite, a type of rock often containing small amounts of gold. The bacteria eat the pyrite because it is made primarily of sulfur, one of their favorite foods. The bacteria don't like gold and leave it untouched.

The technology of mining gold with bacteria has been around for decades, but its popularity is increasing. The bacteria, gold ore, water, and nutrients for the bacteria are mixed in a huge tank in an industrial plant. After the bacteria consume the sulfur, the solution needs to be treated with additional chemicals, such as cyanide. Since the dangerous chemicals are confined to the tank, this type of mining is thought to be less dangerous than traditional cyanidation that occurs at the mine site.

The Unethical Quest for Gold

Man's quest for gold has resulted in war, death, destruction, and despicable acts of violence. Perhaps the best-known examples come from the history of Spanish conquistadores in the Americas during the sixteenth century. When they arrived in the New World, they battled the indigenous peoples over their gold and silver. Parts of Mexico, Peru, and Bolivia were rich with these precious metals. Using more advanced weapons, including firearms, the conquistadores overwhelmed the indigenous peoples. Their populations were decimated, and many of those who weren't killed were forced to work in silver or gold mines. Meanwhile, the conquistadores shipped much of their gold back to the Spanish king, helping Spain become one of the wealthiest and most powerful countries in the world.

Gold Alloys

In nature, gold is rarely found in its pure form. It is usually combined with other metals, such as silver. These mixtures of two or more metals are called alloys. Because the properties of gold are different from those of other metals, it is relatively easy to separate the metals in an alloy.

An alloy is a mixture and not a compound. This means that the elements in the mixture do not combine in fixed ratios. In a compound like water, hydrogen and oxygen atoms always combine in a ratio of two to

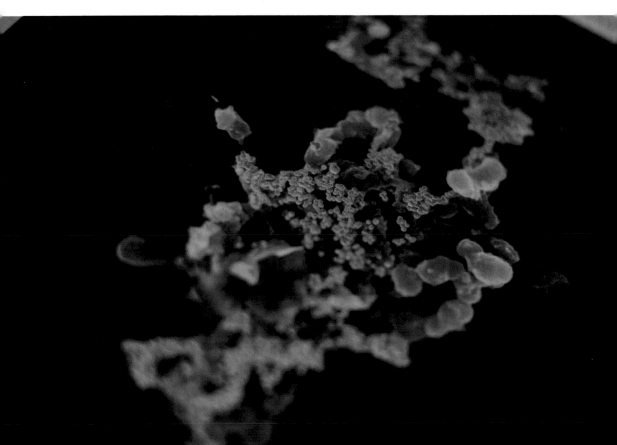

This bacteria actually poops gold. When fed gold chloride, pure gold is left behind as a waste product.

one. However, in an alloy, atoms can combine in nearly any ratio.

Gold from Plants

Gold exists in small amounts in Earth's soil. When plants take up nutrients and water from the soil, they also take up tiny amounts of gold. Leaf mustard takes up more gold than most plants and may be used as a gold-gathering crop in the future. There is, however, a good chance that the plants will not contain enough gold to cover the cost of growing and maintaining them.

Gold from the Ocean

The world's oceans contain over a trillion dollars' worth of gold. This fact inspired German chemist Fritz Haber (1868–1934) to attempt to mine the oceans for gold. He hoped that his profits would help his country pay off its debts from World War I (1914–1918). In the end, the cost proved greater than the value of the gold he could extract.

Pooping Gold

Michigan State University researchers have discovered a bacteria that can seemingly poop small quantities of gold. Assistant professor Kazem Kashefi and associate professor Adam Brown have used the bacteria *Cupriavidus metallidurans* to turn gold chloride into 99.9 percent pure gold.

The bacteria consume the gold chloride and leave nearly pure gold behind when they poop. Kashefi calls it "microbial alchemy," turning something that has no value into a solid, precious metal. It takes about a week for the transformation to happen, and the amount of gold left behind is small, but who knows what the future might bring?

5

Useful and Versatile

///

Gold's properties make it one of the most useful of all the metals. From jewelry to dentistry, gold turns up in some unexpected places. There's probably even gold in the computer this book was written on!

All That Glitters

Gold's ability to be bent and shaped into intricate designs makes it a favorite of jewelers and people who wear fine jewelry. Unlike gold, other metals react with the oxygen in the air in a process known as corrosion. The Statue of Liberty is made of copper, but she was once reddish-brown in color—not green. That green is called a patina; it's evidence of corrosion.

Had the Statue of Liberty been made out of gold, it would still be as shiny and golden today as the day it was created. In 1986, the city of New York decided to cover the torch in gold. The golden torch will shine brightly and never dull as long as the statue exists.

The same properties that make gold an ideal metal for jewelry also make it an ideal metal for coins. Gold, along with copper and silver, have been traditionally known as the coinage metals. Gold coins are not presently used as money but are bought by collectors. The

Gold has been used to make all kinds of items,
such as jewelry, watches, and coins.

value of a gold coin will fluctuate over time depending on the market price of gold and the demand for the coin among other collectors.

Karats

Most gold used to make jewelry and coins is not 100 percent pure. Pure gold is just too soft and would twist out of shape too easily. To solve this problem, jewelers usually use an alloy of gold and another metal. Often, the other metal is silver or copper.

To measure the purity of gold, jewelers use the "karat." Twenty-four-karat gold is pure gold. Eighteen-karat gold is 75 percent pure, while twelve-karat gold is 50 percent pure. To determine the percentage of pure gold in a sample, divide the number of karats by 24 and then multiply by 100.

Medical Uses for Gold

Gold sodium thiomalate, also known as myocrisin, is a compound made of gold, sodium, oxygen, and sulfur, and was initially used as a drug to treat tuberculosis. Although it wasn't very effective in treating this disease, doctors accidentally discovered myocrisin helped reduce the symptoms of arthritis.

Gold in Dentistry

Ancient Egyptians made dental bridges, securing them in the mouth with gold wires. Today, dentists use more than 60 tons (54 metric tons) of gold every year. Gold used in dentistry is always alloyed with other metals, silver, palladium, copper, and zinc. Gold is the main ingredient because it will not react with any bodily fluid or anything put into the mouth. Also, if the dental work was to accidentally be swallowed, the patient wouldn't be harmed. Gold is completely nontoxic inside the body.

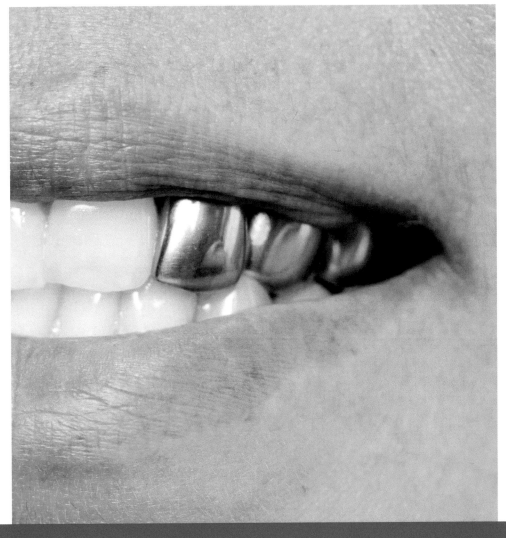

Gold is nontoxic in the human body, so it is especially popular when it comes to dental implants.

Gold in Your Pocket

Electronic circuits in telephones, TVs, disc players, computers, automobiles, computerized wheelchairs, and communications satellites often use tiny bits of gold. Gold conducts electricity very well, both at very high and low temperatures. It also is resistant to corrosion, so it will last a long time. In any electronic device where performance is critical, there's a good chance there is gold. In one ton of smartphones (ten thousand phones), you might recover 10 troy ounces of gold.

Gold is especially popular for more complex dental work such as inlays, crowns, and bridges. These procedures require an alloy that can be molded for the specific patient, but is also strong.

Future Uses of Gold

For centuries, gold's unique properties have made it a very popular element. Gold is a favorite material of jewelry makers, artists, chemists, dentists, manufacturers, engineers, and scientists.

In the future, the need for gold is likely to increase as people discover new uses for it. As the need for gold increases, gold recycling will become even more important. Computers, telephones, and other electronic devices will probably be stripped of their gold when they are no longer useful. Even though each of these devices only has a tiny bit of gold inside them, the gold can add up when thousands of these devices are recycled.

Its many uses make gold an element with a bright future. Recycling gold will make its future even brighter.

Glossary

alloy A mixture of two or more metals.

atom The smallest unit of an element. The atom itself is made out of electrons, protons, and neutrons.

compound A substance made up of two or more elements bound together by chemical bonds. The elements in a compound combine in fixed ratios, such as two atoms to one, or three to two, etc.

conduct To allow something to pass through.

corrosion A chemical reaction that results in the deterioration of a metal. Often, metals corrode when they react with oxygen in the air, a process known as oxidation.

density The mass of a sample divided by its volume.

ductile Capable of being stretched into a wire.

karat A measure of the purity of gold. Pure gold is 24 karats.

lode An area that contains large amounts of metal sandwiched between layers of rock.

neutron A particle without charge that is part of the nucleus of most atoms.

ore Rock that contains a valuable metal or mineral.

proton A positively charged particle that is part of the nucleus of an atom.

troy weight A system of measure used for precious metals.

valence electron An electron in the outer shell of an atom.

Further Reading

Books

Baby Professor. *The Periodic Table of Elements—Post Transition Metals, Metalloids and Nonmetals*. Children's Chemistry Book, Baby Professor, 2017

Callery, Sean, and Miranda Smith. *The Periodic Table*. New York, NY: Scholastic Nonfiction, 2017.

DK. *The Elements Book: A Visual Encyclopedia of the Periodic Table*. New York, NY: DK Children, 2017.

Green, Joey. *The Electric Pickle: 50 Experiments from the Periodic Table, from Aluminum to Zinc*. Chicago, IL: Chicago Review Press, 2017.

Hulick, Kathryn. *Gold (Chemistry of Everyday Elements)*. Broomall, PA: Mason Crest, 2017.

Websites

Britannica Kids

kids.britannica.com/kids/article/gold/353190

Dig deep to learn the shiny secrets of gold!

Ducksters

www.ducksters.com/science/chemistry/gold.php

Explore gold and the rest of the elements!

Easy Science for Kids

easyscienceforkids.com/best-gold-element-video-for-kids/

A fun video about gold, including a list of facts!

Bibliography

Atkins, P. W. *The Periodic Kingdom: A Journey into the Land of the Chemical Elements.* New York, NY: Basic Books, 1995.

Ball, Philip. *The Ingredients: A Guided Tour of the Elements.* Oxford, UK: Oxford University Press, 2002.

Barrett, Jack. *Atomic Structure and Periodicity.* Hoboken, NJ: Wiley, 2002.

Battison, Leila. "Meteorites Delivered Gold to Earth." BBC News, Science & Environment. Retrieved February 22, 2018. http://www.bbc.com/news/science-environment-14827624.

Binns, Correy, "How Much Gold Is in Ft. Knox?" Live Science. Retrieved February 22, 2018. https://www.livescience.com/32328-how-much-gold-is-in-fort-knox.html

Bland, Alastair. "The Environmental Disaster That Is the Gold Industry." The Smithsonian, February 14, 2014. https://www.smithsonianmag.com/science-nature/environmental-disaster-gold-industry-180949762.

Cairoli, Sarah. "Effects of Gold Mining on the Environment." Sciencing.com, January 9, 2018. https://sciencing.com/facts-5218981-effects-gold-mining-environment.html.

Cartwright, Mark. "Gold in Antiquity." Ancient History Encyclopedia, April 2014. https://www.ancient.eu/gold.

Diaz, Jesus. "Researchers Discover Bacteria That Produces Pure Gold." Gizmodo. Retrieved February 2018. https://gizmodo.com/5948739/researchers-discover-bacteria-that-can-produce-pure-gold.

Emsley, John. *Nature's Building Blocks: An A-Z Guide to the Elements*. Oxford, UK: Oxford University Press, 2001.

Gold Institute. "Nothing Works Like Gold." Retrieved August 3, 2005. http://www.goldinstitute.org.

Jamasmie, Cecilia. "Freeport to Yield Control of Giant Grasberg Copper Mine to Indonesia". Mining.com, August 29, 2017. http://www.mining.com/freeport-to-yield-control-of-giant-grasberg-copper-mine-to-indonesia.

Krauss, Gregory. "Can Recycling Gold Help the Metal Regain Its Luster?" Greenbiz, August 27, 2013. https://www.greenbiz.com/blog/2013/08/27/can-recycling-gold-help-metal-regain-its-environmental.

Montana Environmental Information Center. "Hardrock Mining: MEIC Passes Initiative to Prohibit Open Pit Cyanide Heap-Leach Mining." Retrieved October 31, 2005. http://www.meic.org/i137background.html.

Pappas, Stephanie. "Facts About Gold." Live Science, April 15, 2016. https://www.livescience.com/39187-facts-about-gold.html.

Pellant, Chris. *Rocks and Minerals*. New York, NY: Dorling Kindersley, 1992.

US Geological Survey, Mineral Commodity Summaries—2017. Jan. 2017.

World Gold Council. "Industrial Applications." Retrieved August 3, 2005 http://www.gold.org/discover/sci_indu/indust_app/index.html.

Zumdahl, Steven S. *Chemistry*. Lexington, MA: D.C. Heath and Company, 1989.

Index